Oxford Read and Discover

Electricity

Louise Spilsbury

Contents

D1420257

OXFORD
UNIVERSITY PRESS

Great Clarendon Street, Oxford, OX2 6DP, United Kingdom

Oxford University Press is a department of the University of Oxford.It furthers the University's objective of excellence in research, scholarship,and education by publishing worldwide. Oxford is a registered trade mark of Oxford University Press in the UK and in certain other countries

ISBN: 978 0 19 464685 7

An Audio CD Pack containing this book and a CD is also available, ISBN 978 0 19 464695 6

The CD has a choice of American and British English recordings of the complete text.

An accompanying Activity Book is also available, ISBN 978 0 19 464675 8

Printed in China

This book is printed on paper from certified and well-managed sources

ACKNOWLEDGEMENTS

Illustrations by: Kelly Kennedy pp.6, 7, 8, 14, 18; Alan Rowe pp.20, 21, 22, 25, 26, 28, 30, 33, 34, 38, 39.

The Publishers would also like to thank the following for their kind permission to reproduce photographs and other copyright material:

Alamy Images pp.5 (Modern kitchen/Lesley Pegrum), 7 (Lightning/Corbis Cusp), 10 (Round cell batteries/ David J. Green), 10 (Batteries/Alamy Creativity), 11 (Car battery/Joe Belanger), 12 (Electricity power lines/Jeremy Sutton-Hibbert), 13 (Computer cables/amana images inc.), 13 (Dangerous wiring/ Pegaz), 15 (Plastic plug and cable/Purestock), 15 (Glass insulator/Henry Velthuizen), 17 (Solar powered laptop/Global Warming Images); Corbis pp.6 (Northern Lights/Mike Swanson/AStock), 9 (Wind farm/Radius Images), 15 (Power lines/ Peter Muller/cultura), 16 (Coal fired power station/ Monty Rakusen/cultura); Getty Images pp.3 (Teen listening to music/Karina Mansfield/Flickr), 3 (Man using laptop/Blend Images/Hill Street Studios), 4 (Downtown Manhattan at night/Tony Shi Photography/Flickr), 4 (Electric bus/Toru Yamanaka/ AFP), 19 (18th Zigong International Lantern Festival/ China Photos); Oxford University Press pp.3 (Woman watching TV/Image Source), 10 (Watch/Dennis Kitchen Studio, Inc), 10 (Camera/Judith Collins), 10 (Calculator/White); Science Photo Library pp.9 (Hydroelectric dam/Ria Novosti), 11 (Galileo IOV satellites/European Space Agency), 14 (Electric cable/R. Maisonneuve, Publiphoto Diffusion), 18 (Firefighters/Paul Rapson); Shutterstock p.3 (Dinner preparation/CCat82).

Introduction

We use electricity every day. We use electricity in lamps, computers, and refrigerators. We use electricity to cook, to watch television, and to listen to music.

What do you use electricity for? How do we make electricity?

Now read and discover more about electricity!

1 Electricity

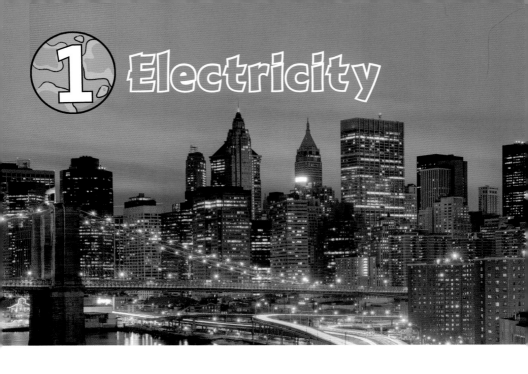

Electricity is a type of energy. Energy makes things work. We use electricity to make machines work. We use electric machines in our homes, schools, and offices.

An Electric Bus

Waseda Advanced Electric Micro Bus

We can use electricity in trains, cars, and some buses, too!

Electric machines help us to do many things in the kitchen. We use a kettle to make water hot. We use a refrigerator to keep our food cold, and we use a stove to cook our food. We use a washing machine to wash our clothes, and we use a dishwasher to wash our dishes.

How many electric machines can you see here?

refrigerator

kettle

stove

dishwasher

→ Go to pages 20–21 for activities.

2 Electricity in Nature

the Arctic

the Antarctic

There's electricity in nature. In the Arctic and the Antarctic, electricity from the sun makes red and green colors in the sky. The colors are amazing!

Electricity in the Sky

Lightning

Lightning is a type of electricity in the sky, too. Lightning has lots of energy. It's very, very hot.

When you see lightning in the sky, go into your home. Lightning can give you an electric shock. That's when electricity goes into your body. Then it can kill you!

The electric ray has electricity in its body. It uses electricity to catch and eat other fish!

How We Make Electricity

We make electricity in power stations. We use this electricity to make machines work.

Many power stations use coal to make electricity. We burn the coal to make water hot. Hot water makes steam. The steam turns a turbine. The turbine turns a generator. Then the generator makes electricity.

How a Power Station Works

steam

turbine

generator

water

coal

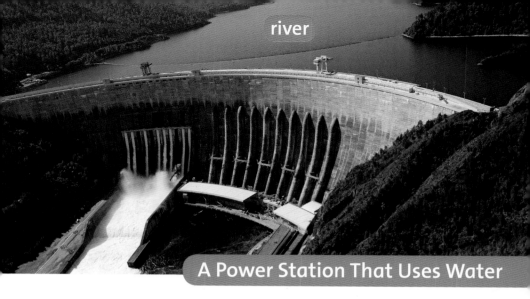

river

A Power Station That Uses Water

Some power stations don't use coal. This power station uses water from a river. The water in the river turns turbines.

We can use wind to make electricity, too. This is a wind farm. The wind turns turbines to make electricity.

A Wind Farm

wind turbine

→ Go to pages 24–25 for activities.

Batteries

Some machines get electricity from batteries. We put batteries into lots of machines to make them work. Calculators, cameras, cell phones, and watches get electricity from batteries. We can take these machines with us when we move. Do you have machines that use batteries?

Machines

batteries

A Car Battery

Most batteries are small. They make electricity for small machines. Some machines use two or more batteries to work. Big batteries make electricity for big machines. A car battery helps a car to work.

Discover!

Some satellites have batteries, too! Giant batteries make some satellites work.

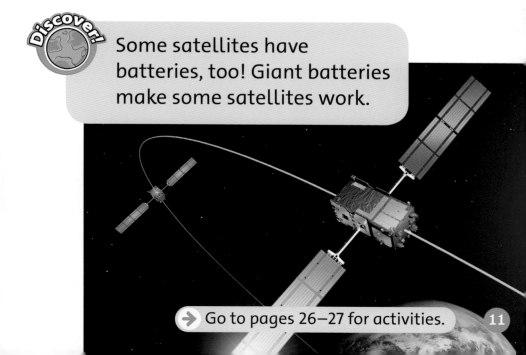

Go to pages 26–27 for activities.

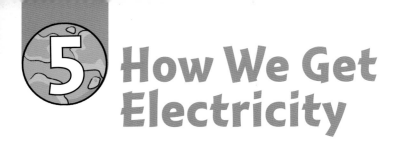

5 How We Get Electricity

We use lots of electricity in our homes. Electricity moves from power stations to our homes. How does it get there? Electricity moves in wires. The wires take electricity from a power station. The wires take electricity to our homes, schools, and offices, too. Then we can use it.

Electricity Going to Homes

wire

plug

socket

Wires take electricity to sockets. We put a plug in a socket to use electricity. Electricity goes from the socket to the plug. Wires take electricity from the plug to electric machines.

It's bad to put too many plugs in one socket. The socket can get too hot and burn.

Too Many Plugs

→ Go to pages 28–29 for activities.

6 How Electricity Moves

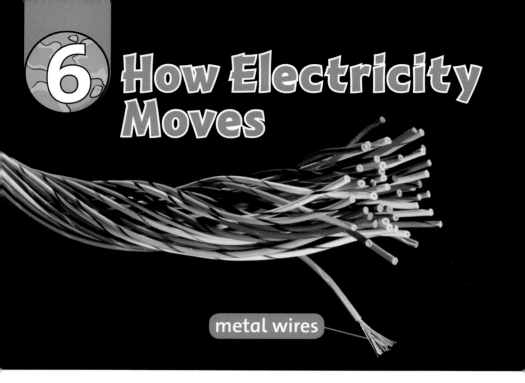

metal wires

Electricity moves through some materials. Electricity moves fast through metal. Metal wires take electricity from power stations to our homes.

Electricity moves through water, too.

 Discover!

Don't touch electric machines with wet hands. You can get an electric shock!

Electricity can't move through some materials. Electricity can't move through plastic or glass. These things stop electricity moving.

plastic

A Plug

Plugs have plastic on them. Plastic stops electricity moving to us when we touch a plug.

Glass stops electricity moving from wires into a metal pylon. The glass stops electricity moving to the ground.

Pylons

glass

Go to pages 30–31 for activities.

7 Stop Pollution!

pollution

A Power Station

Many power stations burn coal to make electricity. This makes pollution.

What can we do to stop pollution? We can turn off lamps, computers, and other machines when we are not using them. We can have a shower, not a bath.

We can get electricity from power stations that make electricity with wind or water. These power stations don't make pollution.

We can also use the sun to make electricity! Solar panels use energy from the sun to make electricity. Solar panels don't make pollution.

How can you stop pollution?

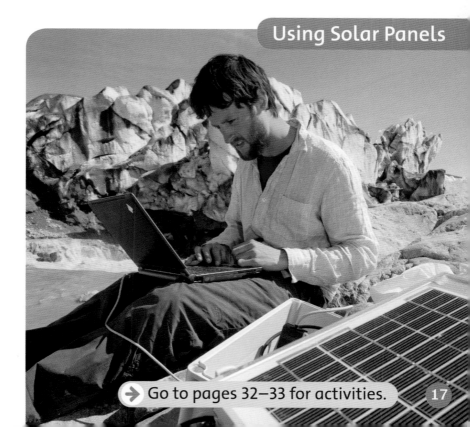

Using Solar Panels

Go to pages 32–33 for activities.

fire

firefighter

powder

How can you be safe with electricity? Don't put electric machines next to water. Electricity can move through water to you. Firefighters don't use water to stop electric machines burning. They use powder to stop the fire.

Don't fly a kite next to electricity wires. Electricity can move from the kite to you!

It isn't safe to put your fingers in sockets or electric machines. Electricity can move from the socket or the machine to you. It can give you an electric shock. Remember to be safe with electricity.

Electricity helps us to do many things every day and every night. Electricity is amazing!

→ Go to pages 34–35 for activities.

1 Electricity

← Read pages 4–5.

1 Complete the sentences.

> electricity   work   machines   ~~energy~~

1 Electricity is a type of ___energy___ .
2 Energy makes things _____ .
3 We use _____ to make machines work.
4 We use electric _____ in our homes.

2 Find and write the words.

b	u	b	a	i	n	s
m	a	c	h	i	n	e
s	r	b	u	s	b	u
t	r	a	i	n	l	i
l	a	m	c	a	r	u
t	r	y	b	a	s	t

1 ___machine___

2 _b_____

3 _t_____

4 _c_____

3 **Write the words.**

stove ~~refrigerator~~ kettle dishwasher

1 _refrigerator_   3 _____

2 _____   4 _____

4 **Match. Then write the sentences.**

Kettles	cook our food.
Refrigerators	wash our clothes.
Stoves	wash our dishes.
Washing machines	keep our food cold.
Dishwashers	make water hot.

1 _Kettles make water hot._

2 _____

3 _____

4 _____

5 _____

21

② Electricity in Nature

← Read pages 6–7.

1 Write the words.

electric shock   sun   lightning   sky

1 _____   3 _____

2 _____   4 _____

2 Write *true* or *false*.

1 There's no electricity in nature.   _false_

2 Electricity from the home makes
   colors in the sky.   _____

3 The electric ray has electricity in
   its body.   _____

4 The electric ray uses electricity to
   catch and eat other fish.   _____

3 **Match.**

Lightning is a type of	very, very hot.
Lightning has	give you an electric shock.
Lightning is	electricity goes into your body.
Lightning can	lots of energy.
An electric shock is when	electricity in the sky.

4 **Answer the questions.**

1 How much energy does lightning have?

   Lightning has lots of energy.

2 How hot is lightning?

   _____

3 What do you do when you see lightning in the sky?

   _____

4 What is an electric shock?

   _____

5 Where does electricity make amazing colors in the sky?

   _____

3 How We Make Electricity

← Read pages 8–9.

1 Complete the sentences.

electricity   turbine   coal   steam   generator

1 We burn _____ to make water hot.

2 Hot water makes _____.

3 The steam turns a _____.

4 The turbine turns a _____.

5 The generator makes _____.

2 Answer the questions.

1 Where do we make electricity?

_____

2 What do power stations use to make electricity?

_____

_____

3 **Write the words. Then match.**

1 w P e o r t t s i o a n

power station

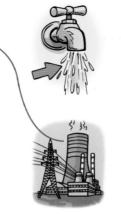

2 i n w d

_____

3 t w e r a

_____

4 i r v r e

_____

5 e t s a m

_____

4 **Circle the correct words.**

1 Some power stations use water from a **tree** / **river.**

2 Water in a river **turns** / **stops** turbines.

3 Wind farms **use** / **burn** wind to make electricity.

4 The **sun** / **wind** turns turbines.

④ Batteries

← Read pages 10–11.

1 Circle the correct words.

1 calculator /
television

2 telephone /
camera

3 cell phone /
computer

4 clock /
watch

5 batteries /
stove

6 machine /
satellite

2 Find and write the words.

cellphonecalculatorcarwatchbatterycamera

1 <u>cell phone</u>   3 _____   5 _____

2 _____   4 _____   6 _____

3 Match. Then write sentences.

Most batteries	electricity for big machines.
They make electricity	or more batteries to work.
Some machines use two	for small machines.
Big batteries make	are small.

1 _____

2 _____

3 _____

4 _____

4 Complete the sentences.

batteries   small   satellites   watches   car

1 Most batteries are _____.

2 Cameras and _____ get electricity from batteries.

3 A car battery helps a _____ to work.

4 Some _____ have giant batteries.

5 Giant _____ make some satellites work.

5 How We Get Electricity

← Read pages 12–13.

1 Complete the puzzle.

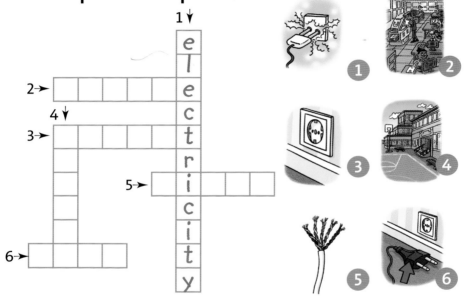

2 Write *true* or *false*.

1 Electricity moves in wires. _____

2 Wires take electricity from
a power station. _____

3 Wires take wind to our homes,
schools, and offices. _____

3 Order the words.

1 to sockets. / Wires take / electricity

Wires take electricity to sockets.

2 a plug / We put / in a / socket.

_____

3 from a socket / Electricity / to a plug. / goes

_____

4 to electric machines. / from a plug /
Wires take / electricity

_____

4 Answer the questions.

1 Where do we put a plug to use electricity?

_____

2 What do wires do?

_____

3 How many plugs can we put in a socket?

_____

4 When can a socket get too hot and burn?

_____

(6) How Electricity Moves

← Read pages 14–15.

1 Complete the sentences.

1 _____ moves through some materials.

2 Electricity moves through _____ .

3 Metal _____ take electricity from power _____ to our homes.

4 Electricity moves through _____ , too.

5 Don't touch an electric _____ with wet hands. You can get an electric _____ !

2 Write *true* or *false*.

1 Electricity can't move through some materials. _____

2 Electricity can move through plastic. _____

3 Electricity can't move through glass. _____

4 Plastic and glass stop electricity moving. _____

3 Match. Then write sentences.

Plugs have	electricity moving to the ground.
Plastic stops electricity	moving from wires into a metal pylon.
The glass stops electricity	moving to us when we touch a plug.
The glass on pylons stops	plastic on them.

1 _____

2 _____

3 _____

4 _____

7 Stop Pollution!

← Read pages 16–17.

1 Find and write the words.

c	o	a	l	e	s	h	o	w	e	r
e	l	e	c	t	r	i	c	i	t	y
g	a	p	o	l	l	u	t	i	o	n
l	a	m	p	o	s	h	b	a	t	h
m	g	c	o	m	p	u	t	e	r	y
m	a	c	m	a	c	h	i	n	e	t

1 c _____   5 l _____

2 s _____   6 b _____

3 e _____   7 c _____

4 p _____   8 m _____

2 Answer the questions.

1 How do power stations make pollution?

_____

2 What can we do to stop pollution?

_____

_____

3 Complete the sentences.

1 We can get electricity from power stations that make electricity with _____ or _____.

2 These power _____ don't make _____.

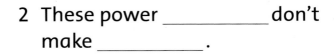

3 We can also use the _____ to make electricity.

4 Solar _____ use energy from the sun to make electricity. Solar panels don't make _____.

8 Be Safe!

← Read pages 18–19.

1 Write the words.

> wires   powder   fire   kite

1 _____   3 _____

2 _____   4 _____

2 Order the words.

1 next to water. / electric machines / Don't put

_____

2 use powder / Firefighters / electric / machines burning. / to stop

_____

3 next to / electricity wires. / fly a kite / Don't

_____

3 **Match. Then write sentences.**

> It isn't safe to put your fingers
>
> Electricity can move from
>
> Electricity can give you

> the socket or the machine to you.
>
> an electric shock.
>
> in sockets or electric machines.

1 _____

2 _____

3 _____

4 **Answer the questions.**

1 What electric machines do you use?

_____

_____

2 How can you be safe with electricity?

_____

_____

3 How does electricity help you?

_____

_____

1   **Write notes and complete the diagram.**

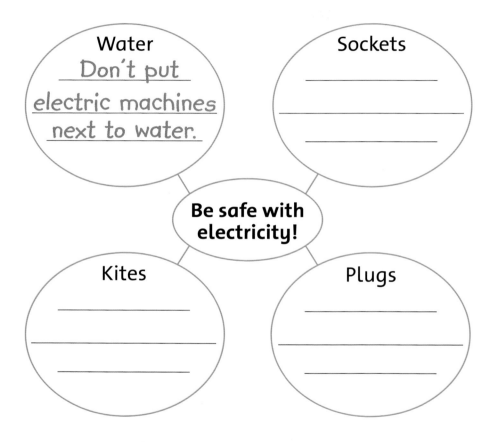

Water
Don't put electric machines next to water.

Sockets
_____
_____
_____

Be safe with electricity!

Kites
_____
_____
_____

Plugs
_____
_____
_____

2   **Find or draw pictures about being safe with electricity. Make a poster.**

3   **Display your poster.**

Machines at Home

1 Think about the machines that use electricity at home. Complete the charts.

Bedroom
lamp
_____
_____

Kitchen
_____
_____
_____

Bathroom
_____
_____
_____

Living Room
_____
_____
_____

2 Write about the machines.

There are _____ machines in the kitchen.

_____

_____

_____

Picture Dictionary

batteries

burn

clothes

coal

dishwasher

electric shock

electricity

food

glass

ground

kettle

lightning

machine

materials

metal

nature

 plastic

 plug

 power station

 refrigerator

 river

 safe

 shower

 socket

 solar panels

 steam

 stove

 turn

 turn off

 washing machine

 wet

 wires

Oxford Read and Discover

Series Editor: Hazel Geatches • CLIL Adviser: John Clegg

Oxford Read and Discover graded readers are at six levels, for students from age 6 and older. They cover many topics within three subject areas, and support English across the curriculum, or Content and Language Integrated Learning (CLIL).

Available for each reader:
- Audio CD Pack (book & audio CD)
- Activity Book

Teaching notes & CLIL guidance: **www.oup.com/elt/teacher/readanddiscover**

Level	The World of Science & Technology	The Natural World	The World of Arts & Social Studies
1 300 headwords	• Eyes • Fruit • Trees • Wheels	• At the Beach • In the Sky • Wild Cats • Young Animals	• Art • Schools
2 450 headwords	• Electricity • Plastic • Sunny and Rainy • Your Body	• Camouflage • Earth • Farms • In the Mountains	• Cities • Jobs
3 600 headwords	• How We Make Products • Sound and Music • Super Structures • Your Five Senses	• Amazing Minibeasts • Animals in the Air • Life in Rainforests • Wonderful Water	• Festivals Around the World • Free Time Around the World
4 750 headwords	• All About Plants • How to Stay Healthy • Machines Then and Now • Why We Recycle	• All About Desert Life • All About Ocean Life • Animals at Night • Incredible Earth	• Animals in Art • Wonders of the Past
5 900 headwords	• Materials to Products • Medicine Then and Now • Transportation Then and Now • Wild Weather	• All About Islands • Animal Life Cycles • Exploring Our World • Great Migrations	• Homes Around the World • Our World in Art
6 1,050 headwords	• Cells and Microbes • Clothes Then and Now • Incredible Energy • Your Amazing Body	• All About Space • Caring for Our Planet • Earth Then and Now • Wonderful Ecosystems	• Food Around the World • Helping Around the World